The Feasts of the Lord
Memorials and Prophecies

Chad J. McCoy

Lulu Publishing
Raleigh, North Carolina

Printed in the United States of America

First Lulu Publishing paperback edition, 2012

McCoy, Chad J, 1972 –
The Feasts of the Lord / Chad J. McCoy
ISBN 978-1-105-64488-7 (pbk.)
1. Judaica 2. Messianic 3. Holidays 4. End time

Table of Contents

Preface ____ *4*

The Hebrew Calendar ____ *8*

1. Feast of Passover ____ *9*

2. Feast of Unleavened Bread ____ *21*

3. Feast of Firstfruits ____ *32*

4. Feast of Pentecost ____ *45*

5. Feast of Trumpets ____ *49*

6. Day of Atonement ____ *54*

7. Feast of Tabernacles ____ *58*

8. Conclusion ____ *64*

Preface

St. Patrick's Day, Octoberfest, Kwanzaa, Cinco de Mayo, Bastille Day, Chinese New Year, and the 4th of July are unique holidays which are celebrated with different types of foods, colors, and customs by people of various ethnic backgrounds all over the world.

While many holidays are linked to nations or notable accomplishments, others are defined by faith or religion. The Hebrew people, although having lived scattered throughout the earth without a nation of their own until 1948, have a rich and storied heritage which they have taken great care to preserve throughout the ages, with many special holidays that are expressions of their faith and unique to their culture. Among these are "Yom Kippur," "Chanukkah," "Purim," "The Fast of Gedaliah," and "Tisha B'Av."

However, among the twenty or so holidays, feasts, and fasts, there are seven holidays of special observance that appear on the Hebrew calendar - not because influential people or committees thought that these dates were deserving of particular honor, but because God Himself ordered the Hebrews to celebrate at these times for reasons of His own.

It's one thing for greeting card companies and florists to come up with a new holiday (Sweetest Day, for example, was invented by twelve members of the Cleveland, Ohio Retail Confectioners International Committee in 1921), but it's quite another for God to appoint a holiday of His own.

In the books of Exodus, Leviticus, and Deuteronomy we find the Lord giving His law to the Hebrews. Among these laws we find such things as the ten commandments, instructions to build a tabernacle and ark of the covenant, and orders to establish seven special holidays along with detailed instructions as to how they were to be celebrated.

"*This is a day you are to commemorate; for the generations to come you shall celebrate it as a festival to the Lord – a lasting ordinance.*" – Exodus 12:14

Other translations put it this way: "*This is a day to remember. Each year, from generation to generation, you must celebrate it as a special festival to the Lord. This is a law for all time.*" – Exodus 12:14 (NLT)

In Leviticus 23:4, these seven holidays are called, "*the Lord's appointed festivals, the official days for holy assembly that are to be celebrated at their proper times each year.*" (NLT)

The expression, "the Lord's festivals" shows that these holidays belong to God – not to man. They are His holidays.

The word, "festivals" means, "appointed times." In other words, these seven festivals were "God's own times." From concept to fulfillment and all of the details in between, these holidays were organized, managed, and coordinated by God Himself.

These times of celebration were obviously of great religious significance, but what exactly were God's reasons for establishing them? What was the deep spiritual meaning of these holidays? What important events did they represent?

For more than a thousand years, the seven feasts of God were celebrated as backward-looking memorials of events which had already taken place in the history of Israel. Passover, for example, was a holiday which commemorated the Exodus of the Hebrews from Egypt.

However, during the time of Christ's crucifixion and the birth of the New Testament Church Age, a curious pattern began to emerge, which revealed a forward-looking prophetic aspect of the seven holidays of God.

In Matthew 5:17, Jesus said, "*Do not think that I have come to abolish the Law or the Prophets; I have not come to abolish them but to fulfill them.*"

Very quickly, the early church was surprised to discover that certain aspects of Jesus' death and resurrection had exactly mirrored the celebratory activities of the holidays which God had preordained!

In fact, the similarities were so great that they could not be missed. Speaking of the Hebrews' religious festivals, the Apostle Paul remarked in Colossians 2:17, "*These are a shadow of the things that were to come; the reality, however, is found in Christ.*"

The seven holidays of God, which to that point had been celebrated only as memorials of events which had occurred in times past, were now clearly revealed as prophecies of a true reality that would find fulfillment in Jesus Christ.

The sequence, the significance, and the timing of each of these holidays (as well as the ritual activities associated with each of them) was orchestrated by God so as to be perfectly synchronized with seven future redemptive accomplishments of Christ, forming a prophetic calendar from Calvary to the end of the age.

The Apostles and other of the early saints were eyewitnesses to the fulfillment of the first four events, which occurred during the Spring festivals of Passover, Unleavened Bread, Firstfruits, and Pentecost in the year 33 A.D.

However, the three remaining festivals of God, which occur in the Fall, were not fulfilled that year - nor have they been fulfilled in any other subsequent year.

If Jesus did not fulfill the prophecies of the Fall festivals at the time of his first coming, it's possible that he may fulfill them at the time of his second coming.

That would mean that the three Autumn festivals – the Feast of Trumpets, Day of Atonement, and the Feast Tabernacles – are prophecies of three end time events, and if a prophetic calendar has been encoded by God within the seven special feasts of the Hebrews, then it may be possible to anticipate – at least to a degree – when these end time events will occur.

Although it has not been given to us to know the day and the hour of the Lord's return (Matt. 24:36), or "*to know the times or dates the Father has set by his own authority*" (Acts 1:7), Jesus taught something called, "the lesson of the fig tree," revealing that it HAS been given to us to know the season!

"*Take a lesson from the fig tree. From the moment you notice its buds form, the merest hint of green, you know summer's just around the corner. So it is with you:*" - Matthew 24:32, 33 (MSG)

In the next verse, Jesus goes on to say, "*When you see all these things, you know that it is near, right at the door.*"

Although many define the term, "season," as a foggy "generation" of indeterminate years, it is also a literal season – and just as Jesus fulfilled the prophecies of the Spring feasts on their exact dates, so also will he fulfill the end time prophecies of the Autumn feasts on the precise dates of the three remaining holidays on the Lord's prophetic calendar - God's own schedule of "appointed times."

What's interesting is that due to the nature of the Hebrew calendar, the dates of these festivals are not fixed, and the date of a given holiday may vary by as much as 29 days.

These dates vary because the Hebrew calendar is based on three astronomical phenomena: the rotation of the Earth about its axis (a day); the revolution of the moon around the Earth (a month); and the revolution of the Earth around the sun (a year). These three phenomena are independent of each other, so there is no direct correlation between them. On average, the moon revolves around the Earth in about 29½ days. The Earth revolves around the sun in about 365¼ days, that is, about 12.4 lunar months.

The civil calendar used by most of the world has abandoned any correlation between the moon cycles and the month, arbitrarily setting the length of months to either 28, 30, or 31 days. The Hebrew calendar, however, coordinates all three of these astronomical phenomena. Months are either 29 or 30 days, corresponding to the 29½-day lunar cycle. Years are either 12 or 13 months, corresponding to the 12.4 month solar cycle.

The problem with strictly lunar calendars is that there are approximately 12.4 lunar months in every solar year, so a 12-month lunar calendar is about 11 days shorter than a solar year and a 13-month lunar year is about 19 days longer than a solar year. The months drift around the seasons on such a calendar: on a 12-month lunar calendar, the Hebrew month of Nissan, which is supposed to occur in the Spring, would occur 11 days earlier in the season each year, eventually occurring in the Winter, the Fall, the Summer, and then in the Spring once again. On a 13-month lunar calendar, the same thing would happen in the other direction, only faster.

To compensate for this drift, the Hebrew calendar uses a 12-month lunar calendar with an extra month occasionally added. The month of Nissan occurs 11 days earlier each year for two or three years and then jumps forward 30 days, balancing out the drift.

Among other things, this variation in the calendar prevents anyone from pinpointing "*the day or the hour*" (Matt. 24:36) of Christ's return, yet the fig tree teaches us that the season of fulfillment will be obvious to those who have learned its lesson – a lesson which begins with the Hebrew festival of Passover in the Spring of A.D. 33.

The Hebrew Calendar

Month	Number	Length	Civil Equivalent
Nissan	1	30 days	March-April
Iyar	2	29 days	April-May
Sivan	3	30 days	May-June
Tammuz	4	29 days	June-July
Av	5	30 days	July-August
Elul	6	29 days	August-Sept.
Tishri	7	30 days	Sept.-October
Cheshvan	8	29/30 days	October-Nov.
Kislev	9	29/30 days	Nov.-December
Tevet	10	29 days	Dec.-January
Shevat	11	30 days	January-February
Adar I	12 (leap year)	29/30 days	February-March
Adar	12/13	29 days	February-March

- Adar I occurs only during leap years
- Adar is called Adar Beit during leap years, becoming month 13

The 7 Festivals of God

Spring Feasts	*Date*	*Length*
Passover	Nissan 14	1 day
Feast of Unleavened Bread	Nissan 15-21	7 days
Feast of Firstfruits	Nissan 16	1 day
Feast of Pentecost	Sivan 6	1 day

Fall Feasts	*Date*	*Length*
Feast of Trumpets	Tishri 1	1 day
Day of Atonement	Tishri 10	1 day
Feast of Tabernacles	Tishri 15-21	7 days

1. Feast of Passover

Date: Nissan 14
Length: 1 day

Nissan

Sunday	Monday	Tuesday	Wednesday	Thursday	Friday	Saturday
						1
2	3	4	5	6	7	8
9	10	11	12	13	14 **Passover**	15
16	17	18	19	20	21	22
23	24	25	26	27	28	29
30						

Passover is also known as Pesach, or Pesah.
Where to find it in scripture: Exodus 12:1-14

The first of the seven annual feasts, Passover is celebrated on the 14th of Nissan and commemorates the deliverance of the Hebrews from captivity in Egypt. This event is recorded in Exodus 12:1-14.

"The LORD said to Moses and Aaron in Egypt, 'This month is to be for you the first month, the first month of your year. Tell the whole community of Israel that on the tenth day of this month each man is to take a lamb for his family, one for each household.

" 'If any household is too small for a whole lamb, they must share one with their nearest neighbor, having taken into account the number of people there are. You are to determine the amount of lamb needed in accordance with what each person will eat.

" 'The animals you choose must be year-old males without defect, and you may take them from the sheep or the goats. Take care of them until the fourteenth day of the month, when all the members of the community of Israel must slaughter them at twilight. Then they are to take some of the blood and put it on the sides and tops of the doorframes of the houses where they eat the lambs.

" 'That same night they are to eat the meat roasted over the fire, along with bitter herbs, and bread made without yeast. Do not eat the meat raw or boiled in water, but roast it over a fire—with the head, legs and internal organs. Do not leave any of it till morning; if some is left till morning, you must burn it.

" 'This is how you are to eat it: with your cloak tucked into your belt, your sandals on your feet and your staff in your hand. Eat it in haste; it is the LORD's Passover.

" 'On that same night I will pass through Egypt and strike down every firstborn of both people and animals, and I will bring judgment on all the gods of Egypt. I am the LORD. The blood will be a sign for you on the houses where you are, and when I see the blood, I will pass over you. No destructive plague will touch you when I strike Egypt.

" 'This is a day you are to commemorate; for the generations to come you shall celebrate it as a festival to the LORD—a lasting ordinance.' "

Memorial of a Past Event

When God freed the Hebrews from their captivity in Egypt, He instructed them never to forget the day of their deliverance. To preserve the memory of this event, the Lord established the holiday of Passover (so named because of the way in which the Lord "passed over" the houses of those with the redeeming blood of the lamb on their door frames), which they were to celebrate as "a lasting ordinance."

Shadow of a Reality to Come

Yet this historical event also represented a future occasion of far more importance: the application of a sacrificial lamb's blood to the door frames of all humanity, freeing the entire world from its bondage to sin.

In fact, this was the reason Jesus was born.

"*For even the Son of Man did not come to be served, but to serve, and to give his life as a ransom for many.*" – Mark 10:45

"*He then began to teach them that the Son of Man must suffer many things and be rejected by the elders, the chief priests and the teachers of the law, and that he must be killed and after three days rise again.*" – Mark 8:31

"*But if anybody does sin, we have an advocate with the Father—Jesus Christ, the Righteous One. He is the atoning sacrifice for our sins, and not only for ours but also for the sins of the whole world.*" – 1st John 2:1, 2

"*Since the children have flesh and blood, he too shared in their humanity so that by his death he might break the power of him who holds the power of death—that is, the devil.*" – Hebrews 2:14, 15

"*Otherwise Christ would have had to suffer many times since the creation of the world. But he has appeared once for all at the culmination of the ages to do away with sin by the sacrifice of himself. Just as people are destined to die once, and after that to face judgment, so Christ was sacrificed once to take away the sins of many; and he will appear a second time, not to bear sin, but to bring salvation to those who are waiting for him.*" – Hebrews 9:26-28

"*And by that will, we have been made holy through the sacrifice of the body of Jesus Christ once for all. Day after day every priest stands and performs his religious duties; again and again he offers the same sacrifices, which can never take away sins. But when this priest had offered for all time one sacrifice for sins, he sat down at the right hand of God.*" – Hebrews 10:10-12

When Jesus said, "*Do not think that I have come to abolish the Law or the Prophets; I have not come to abolish them but to fulfill them,*" (Matt. 5:17) he was proclaiming that through him, much prophesy would soon be fulfilled.

A Divine Plan

Much of what happened to the Hebrews throughout history occurred by design: their triumphs and failures, their captivities and deliverances, their blessings and curses, their wealth and poverty.

These were threads in a masterfully woven tapestry that combine to tell a story that is grander than the sum of its parts. When viewed in its entirety, the greater picture revealed is that of mankind's fall from grace and the reconciliation made possible by "*the lamb who was slaughtered before the creation of the world.*" - Rev. 13:8 (GWT)

Imagine a camera that has zoomed in close to reveal a line on a piece of paper. What does that line represent? At this level of magnification, we can't tell. It could be anything – part of a word, a picture, a number, a meaningless mark made by a careless hand that unconsciously bumped a pencil against the paper, a flaw in the manufacturing process of the paper, or perhaps something else.

When the camera reduces its level of magnification by a degree, however, we see that the small stroke was part of a letter of the alphabet – perhaps it was a line of printing or a cursive swirl.

When the camera pulls back farther still, we can see that this letter is just one of many, and together these letters form a larger word.

Pull the camera back another level, and that word is joined by many other words creating a sentence, and that sentence is but one in a chapter, and that chapter but one in a larger story.

When finally the camera reduces its magnification completely, we see that this is just one story among many in a series which recounts an epic tale.

In just the same way, the triumphs and tribulations of the Hebrews weave together an illustration over the centuries that culminates in the grand story of the Gospel – the death, burial, and resurrection of Jesus Christ which provides mankind once and forever with a means of reconciliation with the Father.

Buried deep within this narrative like silver threads in a rich tapestry, the Hebraic feasts can be found underpinning this epic saga of mankind's bondage to sin and redemption through Christ.

When the Hebrews were following Moses on their way out of Egypt, no one had any idea that this event was actually a prophetic shadow of a reality which would later be expressed through Jesus Christ. When they passed through the Red Sea, they weren't conscious of the fact that this act was a shadow of baptism that the Messiah would model as an example for them to follow in order to receive forgiveness for their sins.

They were far too focused on their current situation in order to see that these things were part of a larger picture. They were too close to the details to see these things for what they were, but as time went on and their perspective changed, the shadows of prophecy would resolve and the reality would finally come into clear focus.

The Passover feast represented more than just the deliverance of the Hebrews from Egypt – it also symbolized the deliverance which the human race would one day receive from the bondage of sin through the sacrificial blood of an innocent lamb.

Fulfillment of Prophecy

The Passover feast was a type and shadow of the deliverance which was to come for all mankind, and when that deliverance finally came, it occurred on the date of Nissan 14 – the date of Passover.

It was on Passover that Jesus was sacrificed for the sins of the world (John 13:1; 18:28, 39; 19:14; Matthew 27:62), and 1st

Corinthians 5:7 affirms that Christ's death was the fulfillment of the Passover prophecy.

"*Get rid of the old yeast, so that you may be a new unleavened batch—as you really are. For Christ, our Passover lamb, has been sacrificed.*"

It was amazing to the early church when they realized that Jesus' death and resurrection were the fulfillment of important feast days that Israel had observed for ages.

Colossians 2:16, 17 affirms that these holy days were symbolic of events which would take place in the future.

"*Therefore do not let anyone judge you by what you eat or drink, or with regard to a religious festival, a New Moon celebration or a Sabbath day. These are a shadow of the things that were to come; the reality, however, is found in Christ.*"

Examining the Prophecies

It has been noticed that many other important events in Israel's history took place on the anniversaries of their holy days. Students of prophecy cannot help but notice the possibility that other festivals on the Hebraic calendar may have special meaning for end time events which have yet to occur, and it is only proper that such possibilities be investigated.

Confused Dates

It should be noted that Passover is so closely associated with the Feast of Unleavened Bread that the two are sometimes considered a single event, referred to as a "double festival."

Even by the time of Jesus it was common to refer to both as one feast (Luke 22:1, 7; Matthew 26:17), as the people "called both the Feast of the Passover and the Feast of Unleavened Bread, the two really forming a double festival." - Zondervan's New International Bible Dictionary (JD Douglas and Merrill C. Tenney) Zondervan Publishing House, page 350

"The Passover... begins at sundown on the fourteenth day of the Jewish month Nisan and lasts for 24 hours. In New Testament times, the Feast of Unleavened Bread, which lasts seven days, was celebrated with Passover, making it an eight-day feast... Jesus' last supper with his disciples was the Passover meal." - The Family Bible Encyclopedia (Berkeley and Alvera Mickelsen) David C. Cook Publishing, page 126

Since these two festivals ran concurrently, many people during Jesus' time called both festivals by the same name. Some referred to the entire 8-day period of the two festivals as the Passover, while others called it as the Feast of Unleavened Bread.

This is exactly what we see in scripture:

"*Now the Festival of Unleavened Bread, called the Passover, was approaching.*" - Luke 22:1

"*Then came the day of Unleavened Bread on which the Passover lamb had to be sacrificed.*" - Luke 22:7

"*On the first day of the Festival of Unleavened Bread, the disciples came to Jesus and asked, 'Where do you want us to make preparations for you to eat the Passover?'* " - Matt. 26:17

Part of the error is historical. After Judah and Benjamin went into Babylonian exile by the hand of Nebuchadnezzar, these two Hebrew tribes combined the Passover and the first day of the Feast of Unleavened Bread.

No one knows exactly when these two observances were combined, but what is known is that it happened during the Exile in Babylon. The Hebrews picked up a number of errors while under Babylonian influence, and the joining of the Passover with the Feast of Unleavened Bread was one of them.

The Encyclopaedia Judaica confirms the mistake committed by these Jews: "The feast of Passover consists of two parts: The Passover ceremony and the Feast of Unleavened Bread. Originally, both parts existed separately; but at the beginning of the [Babylonian] exile they were combined." Vol. 13, page 169.

"The Passover and the Feast of Unleavened Bread rituals were originally two separate observances which were combined sometime between the events of the Exodus and the redaction of the text." - "The Torah," by W. Gunther Plaunt, page 445.

While these two distinct holidays were merged together and commonly thought of as a single holiday even during the time of Jesus, they were originally instituted by God as two separate feasts: Passover, which occurred on Nissan 14, and the seven-day Feast of Unleavened Bread, which began on Nissan 15.

Hebrew Time

The Hebrew calendar is different from the Gregorian calendar which we use, and a proper understanding of how to calculate dates according to the Hebrew calendar is going to be extremely important in understanding the feasts of Passover and Unleavened Bread.

The Hebrew calendar has only 360 days rather than 365, and each day begins at sundown, rather than midnight.

The basis for such a calendar can be found in scripture. It's recorded in Genesis that when God created each day, He defined it as "the evening and the morning," beginning with the evening and night hours and then the morning and daylight hours.

In Leviticus 23:32, God commanded the Hebrews, "*From the evening of the ninth day of the month until the following evening you are to observe your sabbath.*"

So the days of the Hebrew calendar are reckoned from evening to evening, beginning at sundown when the new day begins.

This results in each Hebrew day beginning at a different time (because sundown comes at different times on different days throughout the year) whereas according to the Gregorian calendar, our days always begin at 12:00 am.

For example, let's say that today's date is the 22nd, and that sundown will fall at 9:00 pm tonight.

According to the Hebrew calendar, when 9:00 pm arrives, a new day begins and the date now advances to the 23rd.

A Loosely-Observed Calendar

This evening-to-evening method of reckoning was the Divinely-appointed calendar which the Hebrews were supposed to follow. However, the Jews grew lax in keeping this system, and even by the time of Jesus they were no longer observing God's calendar with any degree of accuracy.

Most Gentiles assume that the Jews observed the Divine calendar just as strictly as they obeyed the dietary requirements and Sabbath laws concerning work, yet there were many liberties being taken with the Hebrew method of measuring time.

Some of these changes were being made officially for practical reasons by the Jewish religious leaders, while other changes began to creep into common Jewish use as a result of Gentile influences.

For example, while the Jews should have always considered the evening and night hours as the beginning of a new day, many began to reckon the new day to begin at midnight, as did the Gentiles.

In other words, if the day was Monday with sundown falling at 9:00 pm, the Jews would refer to 10:00 pm as "later that Monday," rather than "early that Tuesday."

Since the Hebrews have always been so careful to strictly observe every "jot and tittle" of their laws and customs, this is a curious imprecision which continues to this day.

Over a period of several months in 2005, I interviewed a number of orthodox Jews and rabbis and asked the following question:

"Let's say that sundown occurs at 9:00 pm on the 13th according to the Gentile calendar. At 10:00 pm, however, Jews still seem to refer to this portion of the day as the evening of the 13th rather than the morning of the 14th. Why is that?"

The Jews I spoke with were amazed to discover that despite their strict adherence to Hebrew law and custom, there was a casual carelessness with regard to observing the Hebrew calendar that goes unnoticed and unquestioned by the average Jew. Those who do notice the oversight explain its existence as a result of having lived amongst the Gentiles for too long and absorbing too many of their customs.

While the Jews may not have been consciously aware of their failure to adhere strictly to the Divine timetable, nor understand exactly where the laxity crept in – or care – the fact remains that they do recognize that an error has been made which results in a different method of reckoning time than that which the Lord gave them.

According to Dennis McCallum in his "Chronological Study of the Life of Christ," this carelessness may actually originate from the fact that "*there were two systems in existence at that time* [the time of Christ] *for dating days: The ancient dating method which measured a day from morning to morning and the official dating method which measured a day from evening to evening.*

"*The need for keeping this dual system had arisen because thousands of people would come to Jerusalem to have their lambs ritually slain in the Temple. If they only had one day in which to prepare for the Passover, it would have been extremely difficult to have slaughtered all the lambs brought in to be sacrificed.*

"*Therefore, they worked on two different time scales. The Northern part of the country went with the old way of dating (starting from morning and going to the following morning). The Southern part of the country followed the official dating method (from evening to evening). Thus, there were two times when lambs were being killed in the Temple for sacrifice.*

"*With two calendars in use, it was possible to spread the slaughter procedure over two days. The Galilean worshippers had their lamb killed on Thursday, while the Judeans had theirs killed on Friday. In both cases, the worshippers were eating their lamb on the same evening that it was killed. Thus, the Judeans were technically eating their lamb on Saturday, even though it was only sun-down on Friday by our reckoning.*"

As a Galilean, Jesus ate his Passover a day earlier than the scribes, Pharisees, and teachers of the law – which entirely accounts for the biblical record of his eating of the Passover before those who crucified him had eaten theirs.

It is possible that this practice, adopted for practical reasons during Passover season, carried over into everyday life and became for the Jews the catalyst which blurred the line between the Hebrew and Roman methods of reckoning time.

In addition, according to the Zondervan Pictorial Dictionary, the Hebrews had by the first century adopted various time-keeping elements of Roman chronology, including partitioning the night hours into four distinct portions, or "watches," as the Romans referred to them. These watches began at 9:30 pm, 12:00 am, 2:30 am (known as the cock crow watch), and 5:00 am.

Evidence that the Jews had adopted these Roman watches can be found in scripture, where even Jesus mentions the Roman "cock crow watch."

"*Jesus said unto him, Verily I say unto thee, That this night, before the cock crow, thou shalt deny me thrice.*" - Matthew 26:34

So there were three different methods of reckoning time in use by the Jews during the time of Jesus:

1. The official method of God's "evening to evening" day.
2. God's timetable, loosely observed, in which the night hours are still referred to as part of the previous day – even though a new day had begun when evening arrived. What's confusing about this is that the Jews may correctly refer to the proper Hebrew date, (such as the 11th) and yet still refer to the evening hours by saying, "later on the night of the 11th," when they should be referring to this portion of the day as, "early on the morning of the 12th."
3. The Roman "morning to morning" day.

These different chronologies are found interwoven throughout the Gospel narratives of Christ's Passion, resulting in much confusion when one attempts to construct a timeline of those events. In fact, without a proper understanding of the time-keeping methods being used, the scriptures will often seem to be contradicting themselves.

For example, according to the Gospel of Mark, Jesus was crucified at the third hour, which is to say, the third hour from sunrise, or as the Romans reckoned it – 9:00 am.

"*And **it was the third hour**, and they crucified him.*" – Mark 15:25 (KJV)

"*It was nine in the morning when they crucified him.*" – Mark 15:25 (NIV)

However, while Matthew and Luke's record concur with that of Mark, John reports that Christ was undergoing sentencing by Pilate at "about the sixth hour" and had not yet been led to the cross.

"*When Pilate therefore heard that saying, he brought Jesus forth, and sat down in the judgment seat in a place that is called the Pavement, but in the Hebrew, Gabbatha. And it was the preparation of the passover, and* ***about the sixth hour****: and he saith unto the Jews, Behold your King!*" – John 19:13, 14

This confusion is cleared up only when you realize that Matthew, Mark, and Luke were using the official Jewish calendar (evening to evening) when they said the crucifixion occurred at the "third hour," (or 9:00 am), and that John was using the Roman calendar when he said that Jesus was sentenced by Pilate "at the sixth hour" (or 6:00 am).

There is then no contradiction within the Gospels, for it is entirely reasonable that the events which followed the sentencing at 6:00 am (in which the soldiers took charge of Jesus) could easily have taken several hours to conclude before the appointed 9:00 am crucifixion.

The methods described here to determine the date will be especially important in the next chapter, so keep them in mind.

Conclusion

On the date of Nissan 14 in the time of Moses, any Hebrew who had applied the sacrificial blood of a lamb to their door frames was delivered from captivity in Egypt.

God instructed the Hebrews to celebrate a feast in memorial of this event, which He called "the Passover."

On the date of Nissan 14 at the birth of the New Testament Age, the sacrificial blood of a Passover lamb (Jesus Christ) was provided for all who would apply it to their lives, so that they might be delivered from captivity to sin.

In this way, the symbology of the original event was fulfilled.

Original Passover Instituted: 1440 BC
Prophetic Fulfillment: 33 AD

2. Feast of Unleavened Bread

Date: Nissan 15-21
Length: 7 days

Nissan

Sunday	Monday	Tuesday	Wednesday	Thursday	Friday	Saturday
						1
2	3	4	5	6	7	8
9	10	11	12	13	14 **Passover**	15 **Unleavened Bread**
16 **Unleavened Bread**	17 **Unleavened Bread**	18 **Unleavened Bread**	19 **Unleavened Bread**	20 **Unleavened Bread**	21 **Unleavened Bread**	22
23	24	25	26	27	28	29
30						

The Feast of Unleavened Bread is also known as Hag Hamatzot.
Where to find it in scripture: Exodus 12:34, 39; Deuteronomy 16:3

The Feast of Unleavened Bread is a holiday which commemorates the suddenly swift exodus of the Hebrews from Egypt. It was an event which began "during the night" and "the Egyptians urged the people to hurry." – Exodus 12:31, 33

Since they had to leave quickly, "*the people took their dough before the yeast was added, and carried it on their shoulders in kneading troughs wrapped in clothing.*"

"*With the dough the Israelites had brought from Egypt, they baked loaves of unleavened bread. The dough was without yeast because they had been driven out of Egypt and did not have time to prepare food for themselves.*" – Exodus 12:39

It was in remembrance of this that the Lord commanded, "*for seven days eat unleavened bread, the bread of affliction, because you left Egypt in haste—so that all the days of your life you may remember the time of your departure from Egypt.*" - Deuteronomy 16:3

The Bread of Christ

If the Feast of Unleavened Bread was actually the shadow of a reality which would later be fulfilled by Jesus Christ, what event was it pointing to?

Since this is a festival of bread, we should be able to find in the scriptures some kind of association between Jesus and bread – and we do.

"*While they were eating, Jesus took bread, and when he had given thanks, he broke it and gave it to his disciples, saying, 'Take it; this is my body.'* " – Mark 14:22

Here, Jesus uses bread as a metaphor for his body.

"*I am the bread of life. Your ancestors ate the manna in the wilderness, yet they died. But here is the bread that comes down from heaven, which anyone may eat and not die. I am the living bread that came down from heaven. Whoever eats this bread will live forever.*

This bread is my flesh, which I will give for the life of the world." – John 6:48-51

Again, Jesus refers to his body as "bread."

"*The Lord Jesus, on the night he was betrayed, took bread, and when he had given thanks, he broke it and said, 'This is my body, which is for you; do this in remembrance of me.'* " – 1st Corinthians 11:23, 24

As Jesus broke bread at this Passover, he said that it was symbolic of his body which would soon be broken for them.

Specific Type of Bread

It's obvious that there are many scriptures which link Jesus to bread in this manner, but this feast which began on Nissan 15 was a celebration of a very specific type of bread: unleavened bread.

In the New International Version Bible, "leaven" is called "yeast." Let's take a look at how Jesus described this yeast.

" *'Be careful,' Jesus said to them. 'Be on your guard against the yeast of the Pharisees and Sadducees.'*

"*They discussed this among themselves and said, 'It is because we didn't bring any bread.'*

"*Aware of their discussion, Jesus asked, 'You of little faith, why are you talking among yourselves about having no bread? Do you still not understand? Don't you remember the five loaves for the five thousand, and how many basketfuls you gathered? Or the seven loaves for the four thousand, and how many basketfuls you gathered? How is it you don't understand that I was not talking to you about bread? But be on your guard against the yeast of the Pharisees and Sadducees.'*

"*Then they understood that he was not telling them to guard against the yeast used in bread, but against the teaching of the Pharisees and Sadducees.*" – Matthew 6:6-12

Here, Jesus uses yeast to represent false or corrupt teaching. In Luke 21:1, Jesus identifies yeast as a symbol of hypocrisy.

"Jesus began to speak first to his disciples, saying: 'Be on your guard against the yeast of the Pharisees, which is hypocrisy.' "

The Apostle Paul explained in 1st Corinthians 5:6-8 that unleavened bread was "sincerity and truth."

If unleavened bread represents purity, integrity, and virtue, then leavened bread represents impurity, corruption, and sin.

The Bible, then, uses yeast (or leaven) as a symbol of falsehood, hypocrisy, malice, and wickedness – yet these are not characteristics of Jesus Christ.

"*Everyone who sins breaks the law; in fact, sin is lawlessness. But you know that he appeared so that he might take away our sins. And in him is no sin.*" – 1st John 3:4, 5

Although there was no sin in Jesus Christ, the scriptures explain that at Calvary he **became** sin for all men.

"*God made him who had no sin to be sin for us, so that in him we might become the righteousness of God.*" – 2nd Corinthians 5:21

"*He committed no sin, and no deceit was found in his mouth. When they hurled their insults at him, he did not retaliate; when he suffered, he made no threats. Instead, he entrusted himself to him who judges justly. He himself bore our sins in his body on the cross, so that we might die to sins and live for righteousness; by his wounds you have been healed.*" – 1st Peter 2:22-24

While there was no leaven found in Jesus Christ, he allowed leaven to be credited to his charge at Calvary in order to atone for the sins of the world.

So what does this have to do with the Feast of Unleavened Bread? Well, let's take a few minutes to look at the customs associated with this feast.

Customs of the Feast

The preparations for this feast are so exact and painstaking that they are begun several weeks in advance of the holiday.

The exhaustive process of purifying the home by eliminating from it every trace, every article, every grain of leaven paradoxically begins by first dirtying every room with heaps of the pervasive powder.

Bread crumbs are sprinkled in corners, under beds, in closets, under rugs, and in many locations difficult to reach with mop or broom.

Every ounce of this leaven is then cleaned up. Walls are cleaned and even re-painted, cooking utensils are sterilized in scalding water, clothing is laundered with all pockets turned inside out, carpets are cleaned and the vacuum bag discarded off site, floors are polished, and all dishes are put away in favor of special china pieces that have never been touched by leaven.

Everything is scrubbed, scoured, cleaned, and aired out in preparation for the Festival of Unleavened Bread, for the Lord decreed that not only was the eating of leavened foods forbidden during this time, but that even the presence of leaven within the possession (Deut. 16:4), houses (Ex. 12:15), or borders (Ex. 13:7) of Israel would result in serious consequences.

No amount of leaven is permitted to exist, regardless of how discreetly it is stored or how trifling the amount. It's not enough for the Hebrews to simply refrain from consuming or touching or looking at leaven, it must be completely purged. Failure to do so is a serious breach of biblical law.

9	10	11	12	13	14	15
					Passover **Bedikat Hametz**	**Unleavened Bread**

After the sunset of Nissan 13 (now the morning of Nissan 14), the father of each household will perform the Bedikat Hametz, or Search for Leaven Ceremony, which purges the last vestiges of leaven from the household. Earlier that evening, the mother will formally place a few bits of bread in several corners or on window sills of the house so that there will be some leaven to be found.

After the service, the father begins the search by candlelight with a feather and a wooden spoon, and the children follow eagerly behind as he explores each room for the distributed bread crumbs.

When he finds them, he carefully sweeps each crumb onto the spoon with the feather and when all have been located, the bread, the spoon, and the feather are all wrapped in a cloth which is tied with string and set aside to be burned the following morning prior to the Passover celebration.

In Jerusalem at this time, the cheerful voices of men and children can be heard from the many bonfires that have been lit in vacant lots and back alleys, fueled by loaves of bread and later the small packages of ceremonial scraps as all leaven is purged from the homes of Israel.

With the biblical command fulfilled, there is now no impediment to the celebrations of Passover and Unleavened Bread.

Bedikat Hametz Fulfillment

Remember that the feast of Passover was a prophecy of Christ's atoning sacrifice upon the cross, and his crucifixion took place precisely on that same day – Nissan 14.

If it's true that Jesus also fulfilled the Feast of Unleavened Bread in some way, then it's clear that the two events would have needed to take place at the same time.

Jesus should have been removed from the presence of the people at the very same time as the leaven was being purged from Israel – after sundown of the 13th, the beginning of Nissan 14.

A study of scripture reveals that this was entirely the case.

Jesus was arrested in the darkness of the first morning hours of Passover Eve, a fact which can be proven by John 18:3 in which it's recorded that the arrest took place at a time when torches and lanterns were required for illumination – after dark.

"*So Judas came to the garden, guiding a detachment of soldiers and some officials from the chief priests and the Pharisees. They were carrying torches, lanterns and weapons.*" – John 18:3

With Passover Eve being Nisan 13 and sundown having already arrived, according to the official Hebrew method of reckoning, the date had just advanced to Nisan 14 and the day of the Feast of Passover had just begun.

Jesus was arrested and removed from the presence of the people of Israel after sundown as the 14th of Nissan began.

The Bedikat Hametz was performed when? After the sundown of Nissan 13 – the early hours of darkness on the 14th of Nissan.

The removal of leaven and the removal of Christ who became leaven for us occurred at precisely the same moment.

It's important to remember that it was unlawful for any leaven to be found within the borders of the nation of Israel on the day the Feast of Unleavened Bread began – the 15th of Nissan.

Yet Jesus, who was crucified on Passover, Nissan 14, was still hanging on the cross as sundown approached.

If the Feast of Unleavened Bread was the shadow of a truth which was to come, then Jesus would not have fulfilled this prophecy if his body (which had become leaven for us) was still there after sundown when the Feast of Unleavened Bread began.

In order to fulfill this prophecy, his body would have to come down from the cross while the sun still shone on Passover.

That's why it's significant that scripture records the body of Christ being removed from the cross just before nightfall on Passover.

"***As evening approached,** there came a rich man from Arimathea, named Joseph, who had himself become a disciple of Jesus. Going to Pilate, he asked for Jesus' body, and Pilate ordered that it be given to him.*" - Matthew 27:57

Scripture records that as Passover evening approached (it's getting near now to the 15th), Joseph had not yet received the body of Christ, but was in the process of asking Pilate that he be granted custody. It still remained for the body of Jesus to be taken down from the cross, prepared for burial, and transported to the tomb.

By the time these things had been completed, it would have been near to sundown, Passover would be just about over, and the Day of Unleavened Bread would be about to begin.

"*It was Preparation Day (that is, the day before the Sabbath). So as evening approached, Joseph of Arimathea, a prominent member of the Council, who was himself waiting for the kingdom of God, went boldly to Pilate and asked for Jesus' body.*" - Mark 15:42, 43

Preparation Day

This scripture mentions something called "Preparation Day." Preparation Day was a day of preparing for the Feast of Unleavened Bread and had everything to do with the removal of the leaven.

Preparation Day is always the day of Passover, and the Day of the Unleavened Feast is always called a Sabbath, whether it falls on a Saturday or not.

This scripture confirms what was revealed in Matthew 27:57; that Passover was almost over and Nisan 15 was fast approaching as Joseph was appealing to Pilate for the body of Jesus.

" *Now there was a man named Joseph, a member of the Council, a good and upright man, who had not consented to their decision and action. He came from the Judean town of Arimathea, and he himself was waiting for the kingdom of God. Going to Pilate, he asked for Jesus' body. Then he took it down, wrapped it in linen cloth and placed it in a tomb cut in the rock, one in which no one had yet been laid. It was Preparation Day, and* ***the Sabbath was about to begin.***" - Luke 23:50-54

Luke reveals that there were only a few short moments remaining to the Passover by the time Christ's body was safely entombed. He says that the Day of Unleavened Bread – known as a Sabbath – was about to begin.

"*Later, Joseph of Arimathea asked Pilate for the body of Jesus. Now Joseph was a disciple of Jesus, but secretly because he feared the Jewish leaders. With Pilate's permission, he came and took the body away. He was accompanied by Nicodemus, the man who earlier had visited Jesus at night. Nicodemus brought a mixture of myrrh and aloes, about seventy-five pounds. Taking Jesus' body, the two of them wrapped it, with the spices, in strips of linen. This was in accordance with Jewish burial customs. At the place where Jesus was crucified, there was a garden, and in the garden a new tomb, in which no one had ever been laid.* ***Because it was the Jewish day of***

***Preparation and since the tomb was nearby, they laid Jesus there.*"
–John 19:38-42

John confirms the testimony of Luke concerning the nearness of the new day. The tomb selected as Christ's burial site was so chosen because of its proximity to the cross.

Preparation Day (Passover) was almost over and the Jews were anxious to bury Jesus before sundown so as to not violate the Sabbath law which prohibited work.

Had they chosen a tomb of greater distance from the crucifixion site, they would not have been able to complete the burial in time.

As a result, the 15th of Nisan found Christ safely entombed outside the city (Heb. 13:11-13) and far from the people on the Day of Unleavened Bread.

The reality of the shadowed Unleavened Feast prophecy was fulfilled according to God's perfect timing, for the leaven (Christ) was removed from its place among men and entombed far from them so that righteousness (a state of pure yeast without leaven) might be attained for mankind.

Christ's Miraculous Death

Paralleling this haste to remove Christ's body from the cross, an effort was also rapidly underway to remove the two crucified criminals from their place of execution.

According to Zondervan's New International Dictionary, "Victims of crucifixion did not generally succumb for two or three days."

Given the date of the crucifixion as Nissan 14, death would not normally have been expected to occur until the 16th of Nissan, entirely accounting for the crucifragium requested by the Jews.

This breaking of the legs was required to hasten death, but it was unnecessary in Christ's case, for he had already died – sooner than was expected.

This timetable was in God's complete control, for if events had been left to transpire according to the dictates of man, the prophetic events would not have occurred on the correct dates.

"There was a law made by the Roman Senate, in Tiberius's time... that the execution of criminals should be deferred at least ten days after sentence. But there were scarcely allowed so many minutes to our Lord Jesus; nor had he any breathing time during those minutes; it was a crisis, and there were no lucid intervals allowed him; deep called unto deep, and the storm continued without any intermission." - Matthew Henry's Commentary on the Bible

Although the law required death sentences to be suspended for at least ten days from the date of conviction, that would have resulted in a crucifixion date of Nisan 24, which would be a week and a half after Passover and therefore devoid of any prophetic significance.

However, God was in control of the timeline of events, allowing for Roman law to be circumvented so that His plan would come together according to His will.

When the Roman soldiers came to perform the crucifragium upon Jesus, they discovered there was no need to do so, for he was already dead. This was unnatural. In Mark 15:44, Pilate was shocked.

"*Pilate couldn't believe that Jesus was already dead, so he called for the Roman military officer in charge and asked him.*"

Pilate was stunned that anyone would die so soon after being crucified. This, too, was according to God's timetable. Although the two criminals had to have their legs broken in order to be removed from the cross on the Day of Preparation for the Feast of Unleavened Bread, no such act was required on behalf of Jesus. All was accomplished according to the Father's time and plan.

The error that must be alertly avoided is that of associating the first day of the Feast of Unleavened Bread with the *removal* of leaven, for that day is not a day of purging, but a celebration of its absence. The purging occurs prior to the festival.

Conclusion

In order for the Feast of Unleavened Bread to have been fulfilled by Christ, he had to have been removed from the homes and streets of Israel and have already taken up residence within the place of burial before the 15th of Nissan so that on the appointed day all "leaven" within Israel would have been removed.

While Christ fulfills the Passover by dying on the cross on the 14th of Nissan, he also fulfills the Feast of Unleavened Bread by his removal from society on the early darkened hours of the 14th, and by his removal from the cross and subsequent entombment on the 14th.

Nissan 14 (early hours of darkness) – Bedikat Hametz / Christ's arrest
Nissan 14 (waning daylight hours) – Passover / Christ's death and removal from the cross
Nissan 15 – Feast of Unleavened Bread / Christ as leaven in the tomb

Original Passover Instituted: 1440 B.C.
Prophetic Fulfillment: 33 A.D.

3. Feast of Firstfruits

Date: Nissan 16
Length: 1 day

Nissan

Sunday	Monday	Tuesday	Wednesday	Thursday	Friday	Saturday
						1
2	3	4	5	6	7	8
9	10	11	12	13	14 **Passover**	15 **Unleavened Bread**
16 **Unleavened Bread** / **Firstfruits**	17 **Unleavened Bread**	18 **Unleavened Bread**	19 **Unleavened Bread**	20 **Unleavened Bread**	21 **Unleavened Bread**	22
23	24	25	26	27	28	29
30						

The Feast of Firstfruits is also known as the Feast of Early Firstfruits.
Where to find it in scripture: Leviticus 23:10, 11

The Feast of Firstfruits occurs on the second day of the Feast of Unleavened Bread on Nissan 16. On this day, two holidays are being observed.

It is sometimes called the Feast of Early Firstfruits because fifty days later, the Feast of Latter Firstfruits occurs (also known as the Feast of Weeks, or Pentecost). The period of time in between the two Firstfruits festivals is called "The Counting of the Omer."

"*Speak to the children of Israel, and say to them: 'When you come into the land which I give to you, and reap its harvest, then you shall bring a sheaf of the firstfruits of your harvest to the priest. He shall wave the sheaf before the LORD, to be accepted on your behalf; on the day after the Sabbath the priest shall wave it.*" – Leviticus 23:10, 11 (KJV)

Seven High Sabbaths

The Lord designated seven "high days" of the year as special Sabbaths (Lev. 23:7, 8, 21, 25, 27, 30-32, 35-36) which were to be observed the same way as the weekly Sabbath of rest, even if these dates didn't happen to fall on the seventh day of the week.

The first day of the Feast of Unleavened Bread (Nissan 15) was the first of these seven annual Sabbaths. The seventh day of the Feast of Unleavened Bread (Nissan 21) was the second of these high holy days.

9	10	11	12	13	14	15
					Passover	Unleavened Bread High Sabbath
16	17	18	19	20	21	22
Unleavened Bread Firstfruits	Unleavened Bread	Unleavened Bread	Unleavened Bread	Unleavened Bread	Unleavened Bread High Sabbath	

In the passage of scripture above, many (including first century Sadducees, Karaite Jews, and certain modern interpreters) have not understood that the words, "*on the day after the Sabbath*" refer to the first High Sabbath day of Nissan 15, the first day of the Feast of Unleavened Bread.

The fact that there were seven High Sabbaths in addition to the standard weekly sabbaths is not always understood by those attempting to put together a timeline of events concerning the Messiah's crucifixion.

Another point of confusion is that there were two days that were designated as Preparation Day. The Friday before every weekly sabbath was always called Preparation Day, yet the day before the Feast of Unleavened Bread (Passover) was also known as Preparation Day.

As Jesus observed in Matthew 23:23, the Pharisees, however, were remarkably scrupulous in the performance of all the rites and ceremonies of the Jewish religion, and these things were accurately recorded and observed by this sect. While others may have believed that the harvest of the firstfruits sheaf was supposed to take place on another day, according to the testimony of Josephus in his "Antiquities of the Jews," the Pharisees properly understood that this was to be performed on the date of Nissan 16 (the day after the first High Sabbath), regardless of whether that day was a Monday after the weekly sabbath or not.

Waving of the Sheaf

This day, the 16th of Nissan, was always the Feast of Firstfruits, in which a ceremonial sheaf of barley was "waved."

This waving of the barley sheaf marked the beginning of the harvest. Of the crops planted in the winter, barley is the first grain crop to ripen, and on this day a sheaf (a bundle of stalks tied together) is harvested and brought to the temple as a thanksgiving offering to the Lord.

This sheaf is called the "sheaf of the firstfruits" or the "wave sheaf" (Leviticus 23:10-11.) Most modern Bible translations use the word "sheaf," however, the priests did not wave a sheaf. The word "sheaf" is translated from the Hebrew word "omer," which is a measurement of about two liters. The Jews traditionally cut a sheaf, beat out the grain, then ground the first of the firstfruits into flour and offered an omer of that flour.

The sheaf of firstfruits represents the entire barley harvest and serves as a pledge that the rest of the harvest will be brought in. This sheaf was offered to the Lord in a special ceremony which began a forty-nine day countdown until the harvest festival of Pentecost.

Ceremonial Preparations

Two days before the Feast of Firstfruits, on the 14th of Nissan (Passover), the site of this first sheaf reaping was selected and marked out by delegates of the Sanhedrin by tying together the still-standing barley into bundles which would be cut down on the 16th.

As the sun set on the evening of the 15th, and the 16th day of Nissan began, three men would proceed to the predetermined site with sickles and baskets with which to harvest the first sheaf.

Before they could begin their work, the reapers were required to ask the witnesses gathered in attendance a series of questions, repeating them until they had been asked and answered three times.

"Has the sun gone down?"
"With this sickle?"
"Into this basket?"
"On this Sabbath?"
"Shall I reap?"

Only after receiving an answer of "yes" to each question can the harvesters proceed with their work, yet the first and fourth questions demonstrate once again the imprecision with which the Jews observed their own calendar.

More Imprecision

Recall that just after the sun had set on the evening of the 15th there were three men who headed out to the pre-determined location to harvest the first sheaf of barley. This harvest was taking place during the first hours of Nissan 16th, the day of the Feast of Firstfruits.

The first question, "Has the sun gone down," was asked to ensure that the firstfruit sheaf of barley was not harvested too soon, perhaps on the 15th by accident. In fact, the question was asked and answered three times before work could begin.

However, the fourth question, "On this Sabbath?" was a reference to the fact that the ceremonial harvest of the firstfruits sheaf took place on the first of the seven High Sabbaths. Or did it?

This question reflected the imprecision of the Jews to strictly abide by the Divine calendar used to reckon time, because the date of the Feast of Firstfruits is Nissan 16, while the date of the first of

God's High Sabbaths was the first day of the Feast of Unleavened Bread - Nissan 15.

Let's take a look at the scriptures in which God instituted these things.

"*The LORD's Passover begins at twilight on the fourteenth day of the first month.*" – Leviticus 23:5

As the sun sets on the 13th and the 14th day begins, Passover is to be celebrated.

"*On the fifteenth day of that month the LORD's Festival of Unleavened Bread begins; for seven days you must eat bread made without yeast.*" – Leviticus 23:6

On the 15th, the Feast of Unleavened Bread begins, and lasts for seven days.

"*On the first day hold a sacred assembly and do no regular work.*" – Leviticus 23:7

On the first day of Unleavened Bread, the Hebrews are to hold a sacred assembly with work prohibited - a sabbath.

"*For seven days present a food offering to the LORD. And on the seventh day hold a sacred assembly and do no regular work.*" – Leviticus 23:8

On the last day of Unleavened Bread, another special sabbath is to be observed. This is the second of the annual seven High Sabbaths.

This makes it clear that the first High Sabbath is observed on the first day of Unleavened Bread, which is Nissan 15. Let's look at one more passage of scripture.

"*The LORD said to Moses, 'Speak to the Israelites and say to them: 'When you enter the land I am going to give you and you reap its harvest, bring to the priest a sheaf of the first grain you harvest. He is to wave the sheaf before the LORD so it will be accepted on your behalf; the priest is to wave it on the day after the Sabbath.' "* – Leviticus 23:9-11

God decreed that the reaping and offering of the firstfruits sheaf was to be performed "on the day after the Sabbath." If the first High Sabbath falls on Nissan 15, then the day after this sabbath would be the 16th.

So why do we see the Jews performing the ceremonial firstfruits harvest on the correct date of Nissan 16, the day after the High Sabbath, and yet asking the assembled witnesses, "On this Sabbath?" The sabbath was the day before.

The confusion comes from the fact that while the Jews should have always considered the evening and night hours as the beginning of a new day, the corrupted influence from their Babylonian exile resulted in many reckoning the beginning of a new day at midnight, as did the Gentiles.

So although evening had arrived on the 15th and the High Sabbath was over, the Jews continued to refer the evening hours of that day as "later that Sabbath," rather than "early the next day."

Hence the question, "On this Sabbath?"

The sabbath was over. Only as a result of their imprecise observance of the Divine calendar did the Jews reckon it to still be the Sabbath.

Christ the Firstfruits

The actual offering of the firstfruits in the temple was performed by the priests during the daylight hours of Nissan 16, following the ceremonial harvest which had taken place earlier in the night hours of the same day.

The significance of Nissan 16 being a prophetic date is first revealed to us by the Apostle Paul in Acts 26:23 during his defense before King Agrippa.

"...that the Messiah would suffer and, as the first to rise from the dead, would bring the message of light to his own people and to the Gentiles."

What did Paul mean by saying that Jesus was the first to rise from the dead? Certainly there had been others who had been raised from the dead before the resurrection of Christ.

Scripture records the son of the widow at Zarephath (1st Kings 17:17-24); the son of the Shunammite woman (2nd Kings 4:18-35); the son of the widow Nain (Luke 7:11-15); the daughter of Jairus (Luke 8:49-55); Lazarus (John 11:1-44); and the dead man who was lowered onto the bones of Elisha (2nd Kings 13:20, 21) as six people who were raised from the dead before Jesus was.

So what did Paul mean when he said that Jesus was the first to rise from the dead? Consider the following four scriptures:

"*But Christ has indeed been raised from the dead, the firstfruits of those who have fallen asleep. For since death came through a man, the resurrection of the dead comes also through a man. For as in Adam all die, so in Christ all will be made alive. But each in turn: Christ, the firstfruits; then, when he comes, those who belong to him.*" – 1st Corinthians 15:20-23

"*And he is the head of the body, the church; he is the beginning and the firstborn from among the dead, so that in everything he might have the supremacy.*" – Colossians 1:18

"*For those God foreknew he also predestined to be conformed to the image of his Son, that he might be the firstborn among many brothers and sisters.*" – Romans 8:29

"*Jesus Christ, who is the faithful witness, the firstborn from the dead, and the ruler of the kings of the earth.*" – Revelation 1:5

There were indeed others who had been raised from the dead before the resurrection of Christ, yet each one of those people were raised from the dead only to die once again.

Jesus was the first of a new type of resurrection – people who would be raised from the dead unto eternal life, never again to experience death but to live forevermore.

In the first scripture above, Paul explains that Jesus was the first of this new type of resurrection. When he returns at the time of the rapture, those who belong to Christ will also be made alive.

"*For the Lord himself will come down from heaven, with a loud command, with the voice of the archangel and with the trumpet call of God, and the dead in Christ will rise first.*" – 1st Thessalonians 4:16

This new resurrection is described in Revelation 14:15, 16 as a harvest.

"*Then another angel came out of the temple and called in a loud voice to him who was sitting on the cloud, "Take your sickle and reap, because the time to reap has come, for the harvest of the earth is ripe." So he who was seated on the cloud swung his sickle over the earth, and the earth was harvested.*"

Jesus was the firstfruits of this harvest of souls who were resurrected to life and would experience death no more.

He was the first in rank, order, and preeminence of all who would be made alive in him forever, the firstborn of many brethren.

The resurrections prior to that of Christ were physical, rather than spiritual resurrections, and those people ultimately died again. But Jesus experienced a spiritual resurrection - a resurrection to life eternal - and because of his spiritual resurrection, all of those who belong to him shall also rise to everlasting life and never experience death again (John 11:25, 26).

This resurrection is the cornerstone of the Christian faith (1st Cor. 15:13, 14).

Prophecy Fulfilled

While it is clear that the sheaf of barley firstfruits was a representation of Christ who became the firstfruits of the dead at his resurrection, there is a significance to its being offered to the Lord "*so it will be accepted on your behalf*" (Lev. 23:11) that must also be understood.

The sheaf of firstfruits was harvested first, and then offered to God in the temple later that same day.

Jesus would not have become the firstfruits of the dead until he was resurrected from the dead. Does scripture record an instance later that same day of him also being presented as an offering to God?

Mary Magdalene is recorded in Mark 16:9 as being the first person to see the risen Christ, and they have an interesting conversation.

"*At this, she turned around and saw Jesus standing there, but she did not realize that it was Jesus. He asked her, "Woman, why are you crying? Who is it you are looking for?"*

"*Thinking he was the gardener, she said, "Sir, if you have carried him away, tell me where you have put him, and I will get him."*

"*Jesus said to her, "Mary."*

"*She turned toward him and cried out in Aramaic, "Rabboni!" (which means "Teacher").*

"*Jesus said, "Do not hold on to me, for I have not yet ascended to the Father. Go instead to my brothers and tell them, 'I am ascending to my Father and your Father, to my God and your God.'*" – John 20:14-17

Notice the message Jesus instructs Mary to give to his disciples. "*Tell them I am ascending to my Father.*"

"*Mary Magdalene went to the disciples with the news: "I have seen the Lord!" And she told them that he had said these things to her.*" – John 20:18

Notice that second sentence, which tells us that Mary did indeed deliver Jesus' message to the disciples.

"*And she told them that he had said these things to her.*"

What else would she have said here, if not for the message that, "He is ascending to my Father and your Father, to my God and your God."

Notice the wording carefully. Jesus told her to tell the disciples that "I **am** ascending," not that he would be ascending at some point in the future.

Some believe that Jesus might have been referring to the time later on when he would ascend into heaven within full view of the disciples (an event recorded in Acts 1:9), yet there was something else going on here.

If Jesus was referring to the ascension in Acts 1:9 that would take place forty days later, then he should have said, "I **will** ascend."

However, the fact that he used the present tense, "I **am** ascending," shows that the ascension was about to take place.

In addition, if Jesus was referring to the ascension that would occur forty days later, what was point in Mary urgently conveying this message to the disciples? Wouldn't they all witness that later event? Before those forty days had passed, more than five hundred people – in addition to the twelve disciples – would see him and associate with him (1st Cor. 15:4-6), and he could have told them then of his coming ascension.

In fact, Jesus would see his disciples later that very day, and yet for some reason, he tells Mary to immediately go and inform the disciples that, "I **am** ascending" (present tense).

The reason for this message and this particular wording had nothing to do with the ascension that would occur forty days later, but one which would occur in the next few moments, because on this very day, Nissan 16, the priest in the temple was offering the sheaf of firstfruits to God "*to be accepted for you,*" and on this very day our High Priest and Savior was ascending to God in order to present himself for us so that we may now be redeemed from our sins and sanctified for the Father's use.

Miraculous Solution

If Jesus died on Passover (Nissan 14) as the ultimate fulfillment of that prophecy and rose from the dead on the Feast of Firstfruits (Nissan 16), then a problem arises with respect to another prophecy altogether.

“*For as Jonah was three days and three nights in the belly of a huge fish, so the Son of Man will be three days and three nights in the heart of the earth.*” – Matthew 12:40

If the feast days of the Lord were indeed prophecies which were fulfilled by Jesus Christ, then there must be some sort of miraculous solution which can account for the fact that Christ spent three days and three nights in the grave during the two days between the 14th and the 16th.

In fact, there is such a solution. Matthew, Mark, and Luke each record a supernatural darkness which occurred during the crucifixion.

“*From noon until three in the afternoon darkness came over all the land.*” – Matthew 27:45

“*At noon, darkness came over the whole land until three in the afternoon.*” - Mark 15:33

“*It was now about noon, and darkness came over the whole land until three in the afternoon, for the sun stopped shining.*” – Luke 23:44, 45

Jesus died during the supernatural night of Nissan 14, making this the first night his soul spent in the grave.

As the supernatural darkness receded and daylight returned, it marked the end of his first night in the grave and the beginning of the first day.

When evening came on Nissan 14, that natural day now came to an end and the night hours of Nissan 15 became the second night.

As the morning hours of Nissan 15 arrived, the second day began.

The evening of Nissan 15 brought with it the night hours of the beginning of the Firstfruits festival on Nissan 16, making this the third night.

As the sun dawns on the morning hours of the Feast of Firstfruits on Nissan 16, the third day has come.

At some point between after dawn on the 16th, the resurrection of Jesus Christ takes place.

The three days and nights of Matthew 12:40 were not a literal 72 hours. A timeline (given an evening setting of the sun at 6pm and a rising sun at 6am), would look like this:

Passover	- 6am
(Nissan 14)	- 7am
	- 8am
	- 9am – Jesus Crucified
	- 10am
	- 11am
	- 12pm (Noon) – Supernatural darkness falls
	- 1pm
	- 2pm
	- 3pm – Jesus Dies (Night 1)
	- 4pm – Supernatural darkness is lifted (Day 1)
	- 5pm
Unleavened Bread	- 6pm – Night 2
(Nissan 15)	- 7pm
	- 8pm
	- 9pm
	- 10pm
	- 11pm
	- 12pm
	- 1am
	- 2am
	- 3am
	- 4am
	- 5am
	- 6am – Day 2
	- 7am
	- 8am
	- 9am
	- 10am
	- 11am
	- 12pm
	- 1pm
	- 2pm
	- 3pm – 24 hours after Christ's death

	- 4pm
	- 5pm
Firstfruits	- 6pm – Night 3
(Nissan 16)	- 7pm
	- 8pm
	- 9pm
	- 10pm
	- 11pm
	- 12am
	- 1am
	- 2am
	- 3am
	- 4am
	- 5am
	- 6am – Day 3

Conclusion

If the Feast of Firstfruits really was "a shadow of the things that were to come," and "the reality… is found in Christ," then there must have been something prophetic about the sheaf of firstfruits and how it was offered to God on the 16th of Nissan which was fulfilled in some way by Christ.

What we find is that the New Testament confirms the Feast of Firstfruits as a picture of Christ's resurrection. Just as Jesus died on Passover as its ultimate fulfillment, so he rose on the very day of the Feast of Firstfruits as the "firstfruits" of the resurrection, in anticipation of the full and final resurrection of all men (1st Cor. 15:20-23). Later on that day while the priest was in the temple offering the firstfruits "to be accepted for you," Jesus also ascended to God in order to be offered for us.

Through his resurrection and ascension on the 16th of Nissan, Christ perfectly fulfilled the Feast of Firstfruits.

Original Feast of Firstfruits Instituted: 1440 B.C.
Prophetic Fulfillment: 33 A.D.

4. Feast of Pentecost

Date: Sivan 6
Length: 1 day

Sivan

Sunday	Monday	Tuesday	Wednesday	Thursday	Friday	Saturday
						1
2	3	4	5	6 **Pentecost**	7	8
9	10	11	12	13	14	15
16	17	18	19	20	21	22
23	24	25	26	27	28	29
30						

The Feast of Pentecost is also known as the Feast of Latter Firstfruits, or the Feast of Weeks.

Where to find it in scripture: Leviticus 23:15-21

The Feast of Pentecost is also known as the Feast of Latter Firstfruits, or the Feast of Weeks. It is a one-day celebration held at the end of the wheat harvest, fifty days after the Feast of Firstfruits – hence the name of "Pentecost," meaning "fiftieth."

The title "Feast of Weeks" comes from the fact that beginning on Nissan 16, seven complete weeks (49 days) were to be counted down, with Pentecost being celebrated on the 50th day - Sivan 6.

This intermediate period of 49 days between the feasts of Firstfruits and Pentecost is called the "Counting of the Omer."

Giving of the Law

Although the Bible never associates the Lord's giving of the Law to Moses with the Pentecost festival, Alfred Edersheim in his book, "The Temple, Its Ministry and Services," states that according to unanimous Jewish tradition which was universally received at the time of Christ, the day of Pentecost was the anniversary of the giving of the Law on Mt. Sinai, which the Feast of Pentecost was intended to commemorate. Exodus 19:1 does confirm that the Law was given to Moses in the third month of Sivan, so this tradition may well be true.

On this day, two leavened loaves of bread made from new corn were waved before the Lord, symbolizing the two tablets of stone which the Lord gave to Moses.

A New Covenant

If Jewish tradition connects Pentecost to the giving of the Law on Mt. Sinai, then a prophetic fulfillment of this is also visible to Christians because it was on the day of Pentecost that the Lord gave us a new Law, written not on tablets of stone, but on our hearts and minds. (Jer. 31:33; Heb. 8:10, 10:16; Rom. 2:13-15)

As the Jewish worshippers were in the temple offering the wave bread that morning, the multitude heard a "*sound from heaven, as of a mighty rushing wind*" which drew them to the house where the Apostles were gathered. There, they heard "*every man in his own language*" declare "*the wonderful works of God.*"

On that Pentecost day, three thousand people were added to the church and presented as a wave offering to the Lord.

The two loaves of bread which had symbolized the two tablets of Law now represented both the Jew and the Gentile, for the promise of the New Covenant was "*for you and your children and for all who are far off—for all whom the Lord our God will call.*" (Acts 2:39)

Prophecy Fulfilled

Christ died on Passover, was entombed on the Feast of Unleavened Bread, and rose again on the Feast of Firstfruits. On the next feast day, Passover, his promise of the gift of the Holy Spirit was fulfilled.

In Acts 2:15, Peter reckons the time of the Holy Spirit outpouring to have been at 9:00 am. Not only was this the exact time of the Pentecost service in the temple, but there is evidence to suggest that this was the precise time that the selected passages of scripture were read which described the appearance of God on Mount Sinai and in Ezekiel's vision. These manifestations of God in scripture were accompanied by thunder, fire, and wind.

It was no coincidence that God manifested Himself that day with a sound from heaven like a rushing mighty wind. It was not by chance that God chose to declare His presence with flaming tongues of fire. It was no quirk of random fate that the Hebrew word for "thunders" in Exodus 19:16 (kole) means, "to call aloud with voices," and that those gathered in Jerusalem for the Feast of Pentecost heard God speak in many different languages. (The English word "vocal" comes from this Hebrew "kole.") It was not happenstance that three thousand people died because of their sin when Moses received the Law at Mt. Sinai (Ex. 32:28) and three thousand people were born again into new life when the Spirit came. (Acts 2:41)

At Mt. Sinai God wrote His law on stone tablets, and on the day of Pentecost, He wrote His law on people's hearts as He had promised He would in Jeremiah 31.

These parallels are amazing evidence of God's careful planning, ensuring that the coming of the Spirit occurred in a context in which it would clearly be understood.

Conclusion

On the day of Pentecost at 9:00 am in Jerusalem, thousands of people who had just heard the reading of scripture which described the Almighty's appearance at Mt. Sinai and to Ezekiel with a mighty rushing wind, flaming fire, and thunder, at that precise moment suddenly heard the sound of a mighty rushing wind, saw tongues of fire, and heard a thunder of many voices.

For these people, there was no doubt that this indicated the presence of God in their midst, confirming the testimony of Jesus as the Christ. These people were added to the church and the spiritual body of Christ on earth was born.

Original Feast of Pentecost Instituted: 1440 B.C.
Prophetic Fulfillment: 33 A.D.

5. Feast of Trumpets

Date: Tishri 1
Length: 1 day

Tishri

Sunday	Monday	Tuesday	Wednesday	Thursday	Friday	Saturday
						1 **Feast of Trumpets**
2	3	4	5	6	7	8
9	10	11	12	13	14	15
16	17	18	19	20	21	22
23	24	25	26	27	28	29
30						

The Feast of Trumpets is also known as Rosh Hashanah, Zikhron Teruah (Memorial of Blowing), Yom Teruah (Day of Blowing), or the Jewish New Year.

Where to find it in scripture: Leviticus 23:23-25; Numbers 29:1

The Spring cycle of Hebrew religious celebrations foreshadowed the coming of the Messiah and were literally fulfilled by him as the Lamb of God through his death, burial, resurrection, and his gift of the Holy Spirit.

These first four feasts were perfectly fulfilled within the time of Christ's first coming, yet there are three Autumn festivals which still remain, and these have not yet been fulfilled. Could it be possible that the three remaining festivals are prophecies of events which will have something to do with his second coming?

Trumpet Day

In the Bible, the Feast of Trumpets was known as the Zikhron Teruah (Memorial of Blowing) or Yom Teruah (Day of Blowing).

While noisemakers and musical instruments play a part in making any occasion more festive, this holiday is built entirely around the Hebrew trumpet – the shofar – and there could be no festival on Tishri 1 without it.

Instead of merely blowing the trumpets to announce the time for offering sacrifices at the temple, this was a celebration of trumpet blowing, and the sounds would be heard all day in the temple and throughout Israel.

New Moon

The trumpets are first blown at the appearance of the new moon on the Tishri 1 to signify the beginning of the feast day.

The Feast of Trumpets is the only Jewish holiday which occurs at the new moon when the moon is completely dark. A new moon is difficult to see, and if clouds obscured the moon, it could be next to impossible to find. In ancient times, witnesses were required in order to confirm that the new moon had, indeed, arrived.

Watchfulness was therefore an important part of this holiday. If the new moon could not be identified, the consequence could have been missing the festival that year.

A new moon is not to be confused with a waxing or waning crescent. There is no sliver of crescent in a new moon – it is completely dark.

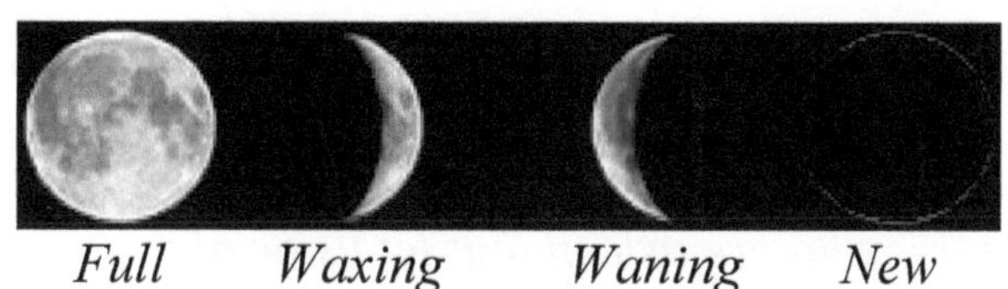

Full *Waxing* *Waning* *New*

As the new moon was especially difficult to see, the rabbis later added a second day to the Feast of Trumpets to make sure that they did not miss it – a tradition which continues in Israel even today.

After sounding to announce the new moon, the trumpets are then blown throughout the holiday in varying sequences and differing blasts: the tekiah, a three-second sustained note; the shevarim, three one-second notes rising in tone; the teruah, a series of short, staccato notes sounded over a period of approximately three seconds; and finally the special tekiah gedolah (literally, "the Great Blowing"), the final climactic blast of the celebration, lasting for as long as human lungs can possibly sustain it.

Fulfillment

If this festival is a "shadow of something to come, a reality that will be found in Christ," then what could that be?

Is there a future event related to Christ's second coming that requires a careful watching and involves the sound of trumpets?

Consider the following scriptures:

"*Therefore **keep watch**, because you do not know on what day your Lord will come.*" - Matthew 24:42

"*But while they were on their way to buy the oil, the bridegroom arrived. The virgins who were ready went in with him to the wedding banquet. And the door was shut. Later the others also came. 'Sir! Sir!' they said. 'Open the door for us!' "But he replied, 'I tell you the truth, I don't know you.' "Therefore **keep watch**, because you do not know the day or the hour.*" – Matthew 25:10-13

"*But you, brothers, are not in darkness so that this day should surprise you like a thief. You are all sons of the light and sons of the day. We do not belong to the night or to the darkness. So then, let us not be like others, who are asleep, but let us* ***be alert*** *and self-controlled.*" - 1st Thessalonians 5:4-6

"*…while we* ***wait for*** *the blessed hope—the glorious appearing of our great God and Savior, Jesus Christ*" - Titus 2:13

"*so Christ was sacrificed once to take away the sins of many people; and he will appear a second time, not to bear sin, but to bring salvation to those who* ***are waiting*** *for him.*" - Hebrews 9:28

A study of the context in which these scriptures appear will show that they are referring to an event which is popularly known as the rapture.

"*According to the Lord's own word, we tell you that we who are still alive, who are left till the coming of the Lord, will certainly not precede those who have fallen asleep. For the Lord himself will come down from heaven, with a loud command, with the voice of the archangel and with the trumpet call of God, and the dead in Christ will rise first. After that, we who are still alive and are left will be caught up together with them in the clouds to meet the Lord in the air. And so we will be with the Lord forever.*" – 1st Thessalonians 4:15-17

"*Listen, I tell you a mystery: We will not all sleep, but we will all be changed— in a flash, in the twinkling of an eye, at the last trumpet. For the trumpet will sound, the dead will be raised imperishable, and we will be changed.*" – 1st Corinthians 15"51, 52

The last of the many trumpet blasts sounded on the Feast of Trumpets, the tekiah gedolah is most likely the "last trumpet" which Paul was referring to, the final climactic blast (the "Great Blowing," lasting for as long as human lungs can possibly sustain it) which will announce the return of Jesus Christ and the rapture.

If this is so, then we know the date of the rapture: the 1st of Tishri.

An Unknown Day and Hour

The problem with this date is that due to the uncertainty of the Jewish calendar, we are still unable to pinpoint the exact day of Christ's return.

Over the next forty years, the Feast of Trumpets will fall somewhere on one of 26 different dates between September 5th and October 5th, and even if we keep track of this holiday every year according to the Jewish calendar, no one knows which year Jesus will return – and without knowing the year, we cannot know the day.

Even knowing that the rapture will occur on Tishri 1, the most accurate statement than can be made with respect to the return of Christ is that it will occur sometime in September, or possibly early October.

It is impossible to determine with any degree of certainty which of these 26 future days will be the day of Christ's return. The only thing we know is the season, and through the lesson of the fig tree, this is exactly what Jesus told us that we could determine.

Conclusion

The fact that Christ performed four redemptive acts on these exact feast days was not lost on the early church, leading the Apostle Paul to remark in Colossians 2:17 that the feasts were actually prophecies of certain events which would be fulfilled by Jesus.

"*These are a shadow of the things that were to come; the reality, however, is found in Christ.*"

With the feasts of the Lord revealed as a divinely-appointed prophetic calendar, we know that three end time events involving Christ in connection with his second coming will be fulfilled on the exact dates of the three remaining Autumn feasts.

The first of these events, the rapture, will occur on the 1st of Tishri at the final blast of the Feast of Trumpets. The exact day of this event is unknown, but it is clear that the season of Christ's return will be the Fall.

Original Feast of Pentecost Instituted: 1440 B.C.
Prophetic Fulfillment: Sept. 5 – Oct. 5, year unknown

6. Day of Atonement

Date: Tishri 10
Length: 1 day

Tishri

Sunday	Monday	Tuesday	Wednesday	Thursday	Friday	Saturday
						1 **Feast of Trumpets**
2	3	4	5	6	7	8
9	10 **Day of Atonement**	11	12	13	14	15
16	17	18	19	20	21	22
23	24	25	26	27	28	29
30						

The Day of Atonement is also known as Yom Kippur.
Where to find it in scripture: Leviticus 16; 23:26-32; Numbers 29:7-11

There are many customs associated with the Day of Atonement, yet according to Kevin Howard and Marvin Rosenthal in their book, “The Feasts of the Lord,” “the modern observance of Yom Kippur bears very little resemblance to its biblical observance. Modern observance is based more upon the traditions of men than upon the pattern established in God’s law.” (p. 126)

If we strip away the extraneous tradition, two aspects of this holiday become clear: it’s a day of blood in which the color white factors prominently.

Red and White

On the Day of Atonement, the high priest of Israel “was required to wear holy garments woven from white linen instead of his normal colorful garments overlaid with the golden breastplate. His linen garments were worn only on that day and never again. The solemnity of Yom Kippur was further emphasized by the increased number of animal sacrifices.” (“The Feasts of the Lord,” Howard and Rosenthal, p. 120)

Blood

In addition to the normal sacrifices offered in the temple, there were ten more offered on this day, including a bull, two rams, and seven lambs.

The blood of the bull was collected in a golden bowl and the high priest took it into the Holy of Holies where he performed a ghastly ceremony.

Dipping his hand into the blood, he sprinkled it all over the floor in front of the Ark of the Covenant in such a way that it splattered, sprinkling it once upwards and then seven times downward as if he were cracking a whip.

The blood of a goat was then taken into the Holy of Holies and splattered about in the same manner as before. Then the high priest splattered the outside of the veil which separated the Holy Place from the Holy of Holies with the blood of both the bull and the goat.

Finally, he mixed the blood of the bull and goat together in one bowl and poured it over each corner of the altar in the courtyard.

On the Day of Atonement, the holiest place in Israel looked like the scene of a mass murder. Blood was everywhere, and yet this was only the prophetic shadow of a future end time event which would be fulfilled by Christ.

What could that event be?

White Linen

The other striking characteristic of this holiday is the fact that the high priest puts away his regular garments in exchange for white clothing.

"On any other day, the high priest would merely wash his hands and feet with water from the priestly laver before performing his service. On Yom Kippur, he was required to totally immerse himself in a special golden bath near the Court of the Priests."

"Five times during the day he changed clothing, and five times he followed the same cleansing procedure. Each time, he washed his hands and feet, removed his garments, totally immersed his body, put on his change of clothing, and washed his hands and feet a second time." ("The Feasts of the Lord," Howard and Rosenthal, p. 122)

Fulfillment

If this festival is a shadow of something to come, what could it be? Is there a future event related to Christ's second coming that involves white garments and a great deal of blood?

There most certainly is.

"*The angel swung his sickle on the earth, gathered its grapes and threw them into the great winepress of God's wrath. They were trampled in the winepress outside the city, and blood flowed out of the press, rising as high as the horses' bridles for a distance of 1,600 stadia.*" - Revelation 14:19, 20

When Jesus returns to destroy the nations that have gathered at Armageddon, there will be such a slaughter that a literal river of blood about five feet deep will flow for 180 miles.

"*I saw heaven standing open and there before me was a white horse, whose rider is called Faithful and True. With justice he judges and makes war. His eyes are like blazing fire, and on his head are many crowns. He has a name written on him that no one knows but he himself. He is dressed in a robe dipped in blood, and his name is the Word of God. The armies of heaven were following him, riding on white horses and dressed in fine linen, white and clean. Out of his mouth comes a sharp sword with which to strike down the nations. "He will rule them with an iron scepter." He treads the winepress of the fury of the wrath of God Almighty. On his robe and on his thigh he has this name written: KING OF KINGS AND LORD OF LORDS.*

"And I saw an angel standing in the sun, who cried in a loud voice to all the birds flying in midair, "Come, gather together for the great supper of God, so that you may eat the flesh of kings, generals, and mighty men, of horses and their riders, and the flesh of all people, free and slave, small and great." Then I saw the beast and the kings of the earth and their armies gathered together to make war against the rider on the horse and his army. But the beast was captured, and with him the false prophet who had performed the miraculous signs on his behalf. With these signs he had deluded those who had received the mark of the beast and worshiped his image. The two of them were thrown alive into the fiery lake of burning sulfur. The rest of them were killed with the sword that came out of the mouth of the rider on the horse, and all the birds gorged themselves on their flesh." - Revelation 19:11-21

Notice here that the Lord is wearing a robe drenched with blood, while the armies of heaven that are following him are dressed in fine, white linen and riding on white horses.

Conclusion

The Bible records this as the second of three actions that Christ will take in connection with his second coming, and it is perfectly symbolized by the Day of Atonement with its incredible amount of bloodletting by a high priest in white linen.

While the exact date of Armageddon is unknown to us, it seems clear that it will occur on the 10th of Tishri in the season of the Fall in some future year on one of 27 possible dates between September 14th and October 14th.

Original Feast of Pentecost Instituted: 1440 B.C.
Prophetic Fulfillment: Sept. 14 – Oct. 14, year unknown

7. Feast of Tabernacles

Date: Tishri 15
Length: 7 days

Tishri

Sunday	Monday	Tuesday	Wednesday	Thursday	Friday	Saturday
						1 **Feast of Trumpets**
2	3	4	5	6	7	8
9	10 **Day of Atonement**	11	12	13	14	15 **Feast of Tabernacles**
16	17	18	19	20	21	22
23	24	25	26	27	28	29
30						

The Feast of Tabernacles is also known as Sukkot, the Feast of Booths, the Feast of Ingathering, and the Feast of Lights.

Where to find it in scripture: Exodus 23:16; 34:22; Leviticus 23:33-43; Numbers 29:12-39; Deuteronomy 31:10-13

On the 15th of Tishri the final of the seven feasts begins. It is a seven-day feast which falls on one of 25 different dates between September 19th and October 18th.

Memorial

For this holiday, many booths or huts are made from bulrushes as a reminder of the type of homes their forefathers lived in during the time of the Exodus wanderings. It also served as a reminder of God's goodness and provision during the forty years in the wilderness –including the manna and quail that He provided for food, the water from the rock to drink, and the clothing that did not wear out.

Also known as the Feast of Ingathering because it was observed after all of the crops had been harvested and gathered, samples of these crops were hung in each family's booth, acknowledging God's present goodness with the completion of the year's harvest.

Prayers for Rain

The celebration of the Feast of Tabernacles coincides with the beginning of Israel's rainy season. The average annual rainfall in Jerusalem (22 inches) rivals that of London, England (23 inches), yet almost all of the precipitation in Jerusalem occurs from November to March.

This means that beginning in April there are seven months in which there is no rainfall in Israel. If the rains in November are two or three weeks late, a severe water shortage will quickly develop and the new crops will fail.

As a result of the intense anticipation of rain at this time, two important customs are observed during the Feast of Tabernacles, including a water libation ceremony and prayers for rain.

Presence of God

It was during the Feast of Tabernacles that King Solomon dedicated the newly-built Temple to the Lord, and the Shekinah glory of God descended from heaven to take up residence in the Holy of Holies (1 Kings 8:1-11).

Festival of Light

Although Channukah is known as the Festival of Lights, according to Rabbi James Trimm, "Sukkot was the original Festival of Lights. The first Channukah was a belated Sukkot observance (2nd Macc. 10:1-9) which is how Channukah also became a festival of lights."

The celebration of the water libation ceremony took place during the evenings of the feast with an impressive ceremony of light in the Temple. This light ceremony was known as the Rejoicing of the House of Water Drawing.

In the outer courtyard, four towering menorahs were erected, 75 feet high, while members of the Sanhedrin performed impressive torch dances. A group of Levites would stand at the top of 15 steps and sing the fifteen Psalms of Degrees (Psalms 120-134). With each new psalm, they would descend another step.

This light display was reminiscent of the descent of the Shekinah glory of God when Solomon originally dedicated the temple and looked forward to the return of the Shekinah in the days of the Messiah (Ezek. 43:1-6).

This light celebration was repeated every night of the seven-day festival, and was so sensational that nothing else in ancient Israel could compare. It was so spectacular that the ancient rabbis said, "He that hath not beheld the joy of the Drawing of Water hath never seen joy in his life."

Fulfillment of the Rain

On the last day of the Feast of Tabernacles in about the year 30 A.D, Jesus caused a great disturbance during the water libation ceremony in the temple.

"*On the last and greatest day of the festival, Jesus stood and said in a loud voice, "Let anyone who is thirsty come to me and drink. Whoever believes in me, as Scripture has said, rivers of living water will flow from within them.'"*" – John 7:37, 38

This was the last time the water libation ceremony would be performed that year, and thoughts of rain were foremost in everyone's mind. Earlier that morning, the high priest gone to the Pool of Siloam and collected a quart of water into a golden pitcher, then entered the temple through the Water Gate. He had just marched around the altar seven times and was about to pour the water onto the altar when Jesus stood up and spoke.

What he said was, "I am the answer to your prayers. I am the Messiah. I can save you now so that you will never thirst for salvation again."

The scripture goes on to say, "*By this he meant the Spirit, whom those who believed in him were later to receive. Up to that time the Spirit had not been given, since Jesus had not yet been glorified.*" – John 7:39

The prophecy of the Feast of Tabernacles was not fulfilled on this day. Although Jesus was referring to the Holy Spirit, the Holy Spirit would not be given for three more years, and in any event the giving of the Spirit was a fulfillment of the Feast of Pentecost, not the Feast of Tabernacles. The Feast of Tabernacles represented an event which Jesus would fulfill at his second coming, not his first.

The Bible records three actions the Messiah will take when he returns to earth. The first two included the rapture and the battle popularly known as Armageddon. The third is the establishment of a Millennial Kingdom, a thousand years of peace on earth with Jesus ruling from Jerusalem.

At that time, the river of living water which Jesus alluded to earlier will become a reality for the whole world.

> "*Then the angel showed me the river of the water of life, as clear as crystal, flowing from the throne of God and of the Lamb down the middle of the great street of the city. On each side of the river stood the tree of life, bearing twelve crops of fruit, yielding its fruit every month. And the leaves of the tree are for the healing of the nations.*" - Revelation 22:1, 2

Fulfillment of God's Presence

After Armageddon, Jesus will establish a kingdom on earth that will bring about a thousand years of peace. This is known as the Millennial Reign of Christ.

"Then the survivors from all the nations that have attacked Jerusalem will go up year after year to worship the King, the LORD Almighty, and to celebrate the Festival of Tabernacles. If any of the peoples of the earth do not go up to Jerusalem to worship the King, the LORD Almighty, they will have no rain." – Zechariah 14:16, 17

"He said: "Son of man, this is the place of my throne and the place for the soles of my feet. This is where I will live among the Israelites forever. The people of Israel will never again defile my holy name." - Ezekiel 43:7

As can be seen from Solomon's dedication of the Temple, the Feast of Tabernacles was symbolic of God's presence coming down to live (to be "tabernacled") among men. With Jesus again dwelling in Jerusalem, the Spirit of God will once more be tabernacled among men.

It is only fitting, then, that the Feast of Tabernacles which symbolizes the close abiding presence of God with mankind will be celebrated in Jerusalem throughout the Millennial Reign with Jesus as the central figure of worship.

It is interesting to see that the Gentiles will also be required to celebrate the Feast of Tabernacles which was formerly a feast only for Israel. In order to observe this holiday, they must travel to Jerusalem once a year in the Fall to "worship the King," Jesus Christ.

Notice, too, that if any nation refuses to celebrate the Feast of Tabernacles during the Millennial Reign of Christ, there is a major aspect of this holiday that will be withheld from them – rain.

"If any of the peoples of the earth do not go up to Jerusalem to worship the King, the LORD Almighty, they will have no rain. If the Egyptian people do not go up and take part, they will have no rain. The LORD will bring on them the plague he inflicts on the nations that do not go up to celebrate the Festival of Tabernacles. This will be the punishment of Egypt and the punishment of all the nations that do not go up to celebrate the Festival of Tabernacles." – Zechariah 14:17-19

Fulfillment of Light

On the day after the Feast of Tabernacles, Jesus returned from the Mount of Olives to teach in the Temple. With the last and greatest celebration of light fresh in everyone's minds from the Festival of Light the night before, Jesus announced, "*I am the light of the world. Whoever follows me will never walk in darkness, but will have the light of life.*" – John 8:12

"More than just a messianic claim, Jesus' claim to be the "light of the world" carried a reference to the Temple light celebration. The celebration was still vivid in their minds. They had just celebrated it six nights in a row. The light that he offered (i.e., salvation, Isa. 49:6) would light not just the Temple, it would light the whole world. He himself was the source." ("The Feasts of the Lord" Howard and Rosenthal)

John was given a vision of Jerusalem after Armageddon was over and Satan was cast into the lake of fire.

"*The city does not need the sun or the moon to shine on it, for the glory of God gives it light, and the Lamb is its lamp. The nations will walk by its light, and the kings of the earth will bring their splendor into it.*" – Revelation 21:23, 24

During the Millennial Reign of Christ, Jesus will be "*a light for revelation to the Gentiles, and the glory of your people Israel.*" – Luke 2:32

Conclusion

The Feast of Tabernacles was a memorial of the time God traveled with the Hebrews as a pillar of cloud by day and a pillar of fire by night as they wandered about the wilderness after their deliverance from Egypt.

It was also a prophecy of a future time when God would become tabernacled among men – not shut up in a Temple where only the Jewish High Priest had access to Him once a year, but in an open earthly city where "the soles of his feet" would tread, accessible by all of mankind.

Original Feast of Tabernacles Instituted: 1440 B.C.
Prophetic Fulfillment: Sept. 19 – Oct. 24, year unknown

8. Conclusion

Over fourteen hundred years before the birth of Christ, God instituted seven feasts which foretold of seven major redemptive events which he would accomplish.

The four Spring feasts were related to his first coming. Passover spoke of his death. Unleavened Bread prophesied of his burial. Firstfruits foretold of his resurrection, and Pentecost foreshadowed the giving of the Holy Spirit.

The Spring feasts were fulfilled literally and on the exact dates of these holidays. The three Fall feasts, which are related to his second coming, will likewise be fulfilled literally and on the exact corresponding dates. Trumpets is a reference to the rapture of the church and the gathering of the Jews. Atonement was a bloody harbinger of Armageddon. Tabernacles represents the Millennial Reign of Christ.

Only God could have foretold of these astounding events and encoded them within His own feasts – the appointed Days of the Lord which comprise a prophetic calendar from Calvary to glory.

One thing for students of Bible prophecy to keep in mind is that the first four feasts that were fulfilled during the time of Christ's first coming were all fulfilled in sequence the same year. Therefore, while it's possible that there may be periods of years dividing the events of his second coming, it may also be that the three Fall feasts are all fulfilled in the same year, as well.

So what are we to do with this information? What value does it have? It certainly does not supply us with dates for these end time events, but it does identify the season they will occur – the season of the Fall.

As each year brings us closer to the fullness of God's appointed times, we can look expectantly to the months of September and October and echo the words of the apostle John concerning the soon return of Christ, "*Amen. Come, Lord Jesus.*"

www.ingramcontent.com/pod-product-compliance
Ingram Content Group UK Ltd.
Pitfield, Milton Keynes, MK11 3LW, UK
UKHW041917190726
13854UKWH00003B/1289